The sun is going down. The night starts now. WomWom may start eating.

The sky is full of bright things. What are these bright things in the sky?

When the night comes it is dark. It is hard to see things. WomWom still eats grass at night.

Stars are the bright objects in the sky. These are suns a long way from the Earth.

The night sky also has planets. These planets circle the Sun as does our Earth. Planets do not twinkle. Can you spot a planet?

The night sky also has meteors. These are pieces of dust and rock that fall to Earth. When they fall they burn very hot and show light.

Our Sun is a star. The other stars are a long way from Earth. The stars in our sky may have planets.

Sometimes the stars look like a cluster. This is called a galaxy. We live in the Milky Way Galaxy.

Some stars are given names. This is called the Southern Cross. You can see it in our night sky.

Australia has the Southern Cross on our flag. It shows the stars of the cross.

Some night sky objects are made by us. These are called satellites. There are many satellites in the night sky.

The night sky contains many objects. It is part of WomWom's world and the time when the Sun is gone.